Exploring
Science
2 
MANOJ PUBLICATIONS

Exploring Science-2

Publisher:

MANOJ PUBLICATIONS

761, Main Road, Burari, Delhi-110084 (INDIA)
Mobile : 09999476076, 09868112194,
            08178823569, 08178854810
Email   : info@manojpublications.com

for online shopping visit our websites:

www.sawanonlinebookstore.com

ISBN : 978-93-5579-329-4

Concept by:
Sanyam Gupta

Edited by:
Rohan Kumar

Preface...

The series entitled Exploring Science comprises a set of five books from classes I to V. Based on the NCERT syllabus, the series follows an activity-oriented thematic approach in which the child's learning is assessed in a comprehensive range of situations and environment both in and out of the classroom.

Each book of the series is divided into different topics. Each chapter starts with a synopsis of topics discussed under the heading Turning Points. Rack Your Brain is an explanation that makes the child feel aware about the topic and relates it to his daily life situations. The content of each chapter is developed in a simple and lucid way, and enriched with colourful illustrations. At the end of each chapter Summary of the Chapter is given to recapitulate the chapter.

The Experimental Work under the heading Get Hands-on Experience and Hands-on Learning is carried out in the form of Classroom Assignment, Home Assignment, Project Work and Classroom Presentation. This will help to link the textual knowledge with the practical experience.

We have made our sincere efforts to make this series error-free, refined and concise. The worthy suggestions for its further improvement are most welcome.

Contents...

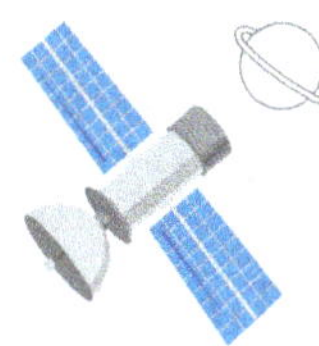

1 Human Structure and Safety

- Bones
- Muscles
- Stay Healthy
- Correct Posture

Rack Your Brain

Monal was going home from school in the afternoon. The Sun was shining and it was very hot. He was getting irritated and thought there should be no Sun in the sky. Then he asked his teacher why we need the Sun. His teacher explained that the Sun is essential to all of us. Do you know why the Sun should be there?

What does the Sun give us? How does it help all living beings? When does it rise and set? What happens when the Sun sets? Let's find out all the answers in this chapter.

Bones

The bones support our body. They are hard. They are of different shapes and sizes. There are 206 bones in our body. All the bones together form a skeleton.

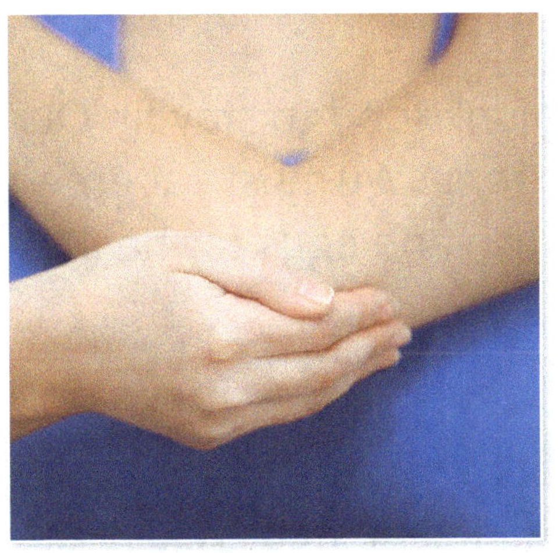

Elbow joint

Knee joint

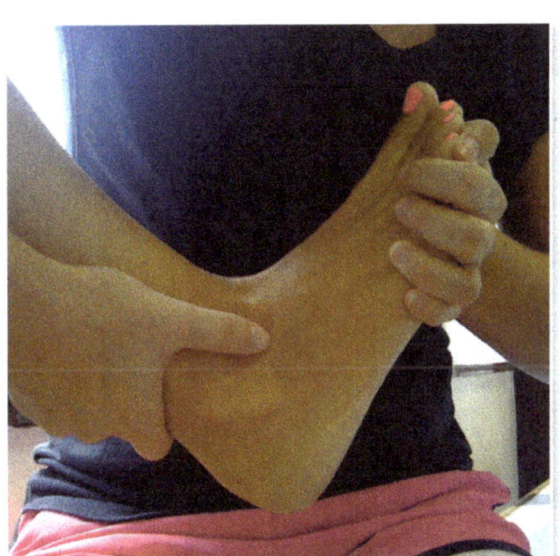

Ankle joint

The skeleton gives shape to our body. It also protects the soft inner parts of the body like our brain, heart and lungs.

The place where two bones meet is called a joint. Bones are linked together by joints which allow them to move in different directions.

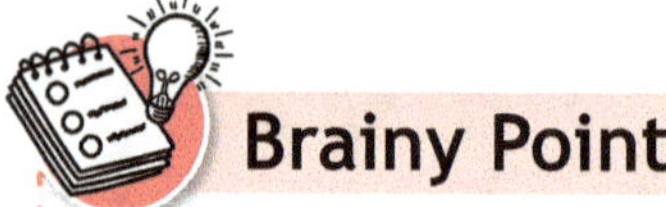

Brainy Point

When we shout or move in a bus or car, it distracts the driver which might cause an accident.

Muscles

Muscles are attached to the bones. We have more than 600 muscles in our body. Bones cannot move on their own. The muscles are attached to the bones to make the bones move.

Bones and muscles work together. They help us to write, walk, swim, stand, sit and do many other activities. Some parts of our body like heart and stomach have no bones. They are made of only muscles.

Our bones and muscles are strong but very sensitive. We need to protect them from dirt and germs.

Our skin covers the whole body and protects the bones and the muscles.

Stay Healthy

We should eat healthy food and drink milk to keep our bones and muscles fit. Regular exercise and enough sleep make our bones and muscles strong.

Healthy Food

We should always eat the right food and avoid eating junk food to stay fit. Our food must contain milk to make our teeth and bones strong. We must eat green vegetables, fruits, rice, pulses, bread, chicken, meat, fish and eggs for healthy and strong muscles.

Exercise

Our body needs exercise every day. Exercise keeps us fit by helping all our bones and muscles work properly. We should play outdoor games. When we use our muscles, they become stronger.

Sleep

We need to have a good sleep as it gives rest to our body and helps us to recharge our energy.

Correct Posture

Posture means the position in which you keep your body when you sit, stand and walk. A correct posture keeps us healthy and in good shape.

Some Rules for Correct Posture

While Sitting

- We should sit straight.
- Our back should be straight against the back of the chair.
- We should keep our chest up.
- We should not bend our shoulders.
- We should stand straight with our back straight.
- We should keep our chin in and chest out.
- The distance between our feet should be about 15-20 centimetres apart.

Good Sitting Posture

Bad Sitting Posture

- We should walk straight with our chest out.
- We should hold our head high.
- We should swing our arms freely while walking.

Benefits of good posture

- It keeps our bones and muscles in proper shape.
- It helps the bones to grow well.
- It keeps our backbone straight and strong.
- It makes our body to work properly.

 ## Summary of the Chapter

- Our body is made of bones and muscles which are covered by the skin.
- Bones and muscles give shape and support to our body.
- Bones are hard and strong.
- The muscles help move the bones.

A. Answer the following questions :

1. What is a skeleton?

2. What is a joint?

3. Name two parts of our body which have no bones.

4. What must we eat to stay healthy?

5. What should we do to make our muscles strong?

    ____

6. What do you mean by posture? Write two benefits of a correct
    posture.

    ____

B. Fill in the blanks with the suitable words :

1. The hard parts inside our body are ________________ .

2. The soft parts inside our body are ________________ .

3. The ________________ gives shape to our body.

4. We should play ________________ games.

5. Our ________________ covers the whole body.

C. Match the following :

Column A		Column B	
1.	Skeleton	a.	Good Posture
2.	Muscles	b.	Strong bones and muscles
3.	Exercise	c.	Framework of bones
4.	Knee and elbow	d.	Soft
5.	Chest out	e.	Joints

D. What is it ?

1. It gives shape to the body. It protects some
    internal parts of the body. ________________

2. These work together with bones. ________________

3. It contains calcium which helps to make our bones
    and teeth strong. ________________

4. It covers and protects the whole body. ________________

Get Hands-on Experience...

Press your different body-parts. Can you feel your bones in the following parts of your body? Write Yes, I can or No, I cannot :

1. In your legs?
2. In your ears?
3. In your head?
4. In your lips?
5. In your shoulders?
6. On your eyelids?

Hands-on Learning...

Draw a picture of the human body on a A-4 size sheet and label its different organs.

2 Food for Good Health

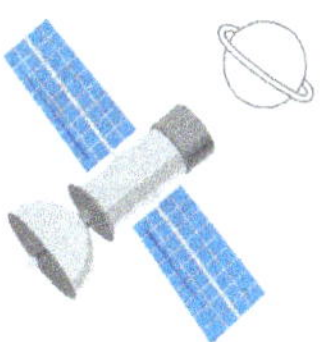

We Will Learn

- **Need for Food**
- **Food Groups**
- **Meals in a Day**
- **Good Food Habits**

Rack Your Brain

Dr. Sharma asked Tom, "What kind of food do you like to eat ?"

"Uncle, I love to eat chips, chocolate and cold drinks," answered Tom.

"You enjoy eating food that is not good for you. You must eat healthy food," said Dr. Sharma, "The right type of food helps you to grow, become strong and have energy for work and play." We all should eat green vegetables, pulses, rice and chapati cooked by our mothers. These foods will make us healthy and fit.

In this chapter, you will learn about the importance of good food and healthy food habits.

Need for Food

Our body needs food because it gives us energy to read, write, think and play.

It keeps us healthy and fit.

It helps us to grow big and strong.

On the basis of our needs, we can divide the food into three groups. We should eat from each food-group in the right amount to stay healthy.

Food Groups

1. Energy-Giving Food
2. Protective Food
3. Body-Building Food

Energy-Giving Food

The food that gives us energy to do work and play, is called energy-giving food.

Protective Food

The food that protects our body from diseases, is called protective food. Fruits and vegetables help our body to grow strong and remain healthy.

Bread   Chapati   Rice   Potatoes

Sugar   Sweets   Ghee   Butter

Body-Building Food

The food that builds our body and helps us to grow, is called body-building food.

Fruits   Vegetables

Every day we should eat some food of each kind.

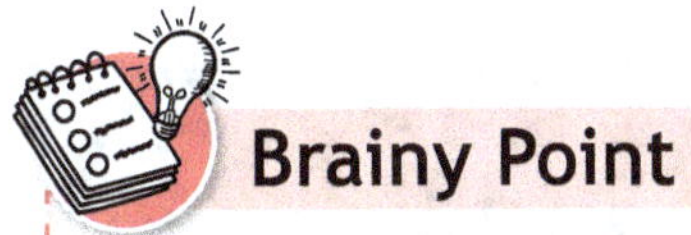

Early to bed and early to rise makes man healthy, wealthy and wise.

This will help us to grow properly, will give us energy and will protect us from diseases.

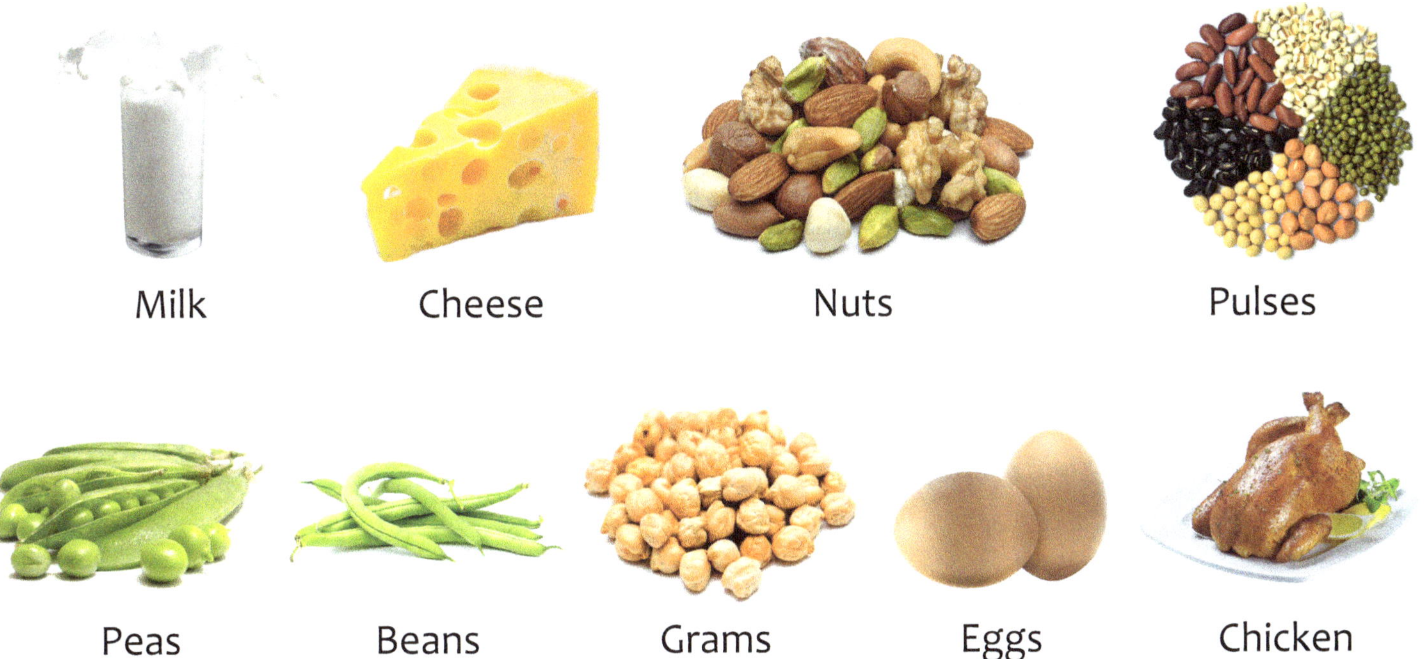

Milk   Cheese   Nuts   Pulses

Peas   Beans   Grams   Eggs   Chicken

Each kind of food in equal parts is called balanced diet.
We should also drink plenty of water every day.

Meals in a Day

Usually, we eat four times a day.

We eat breakfast in the morning.

We eat lunch at noon.

We take milk and some snacks in the evening.

And we take dinner at night. It is the last meal of the day.

We should not eat in between meals.

Good Food Habits

Good food habits are necessary for good health.
Develop the following food habits:

1. Wash your hands with soap and water before and after eating food.

2. Eat food at proper meal times.

3. Do not overeat.

4. Do not eat too little.

5. Wash fruits and vegetables well before eating.

6. Eat slowly and chew your food well.

7. Clean your mouth after eating.

8. Eat only fresh and covered food.

9. Do not buy food from roadside vendors.

10. Eat in a clean place.

11. Do not eat stale food.

12. Drink clean and plenty of water.

13. Follow table manners while eating.

14. Do not speak while eating.

15. Do not waste food.

 **Summary of the Chapter**

- Food is one of our basic needs.
- There are three food groups – energy-giving food, protective food and body-building food.
- Food gives us energy, helps us to grow and protects us from diseases.
- We should eat atleast four times a day.
- We should develop healthy food habits.

A. Answer the following questions :

1. What does food give us?

2. What do you mean by energy-giving food?

3. What is protective food?

4. What is body-building food?

5. Write any three good food habits.

B. Fill in the blanks with the suitable words :

1. We should avoid _______________ food.

2. Food gives us _______________ to read, write, think and play.

3. Each kind of food in equal parts is called _______________.

4. Do not eat _______________ meals.

5. Do not _______________ while eating

C. Give two examples for each :

1. Body-building food _______________ _______________.

2. Energy-giving food _______________ _______________.

3. Protective food _______________ _______________.

Look at what Raj, Sonam and Nyra had for breakfast, lunch and dinner respectively.

	Breakfast	Lunch	Dinner
Raj	Bread-Butter, Apple, Milk, Egg	Chapati, Potato, Dal, Curd, Salad	Rice, Rajma, Salad
Sonam	Idli-Sambhar, Orange	Rice, Sambhar, Brinjal	Chapati, Paneer, Curd
Nyra	Prantha, Pickle, Milk, Papaya	Poori, Chana, Salad, Curd	Parantha, Dal, Okra

Now, make a plate of food for yourself. You may choose the food eaten by Raj, Sonam and Nyra.

Breakfast : ___________________

Lunch/Dinner : ___________________

  Hands-on Learning...

Paste the pictures of different food-items that are cooked by your mom.

3 Safety Rules

- Safety Rules at Home
- Safety Rules in the Playground
- Safety Rules on the Road
- Safety Rules While Riding the Bus
- Safety Rules While Boating and Swimming
- Safety Rules While Celebrating Festivals

Rack Your Brain

Dear children! This is a traffic signal. It controls the traffic. It says 'Go' at Green, 'Wait' at Yellow and 'Stop' at Red. We should follow the traffic light signals. We must cross the road only at the zebra crossing.

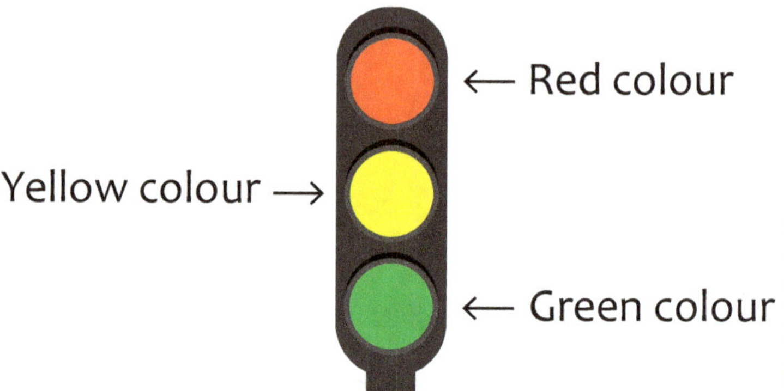

Safety Rules At Home

We spend most of our time at home. There are many things which are useful to us in our daily work. But they can be dangerous too, as we do not know the proper way of using them. We should be careful with them.

Electrical Appliances

We should use the electrical appliances wisely and properly; otherwise, they can be dangerous for us. We should not touch an electrical wire or a switch with wet hands. We should also not touch the electric poles while walking on the road. We may get an electric shock.

Tools

We should be careful while using the hand tools such as axes, hammers, saws, screwdrivers, drill machines, etc.

Sharp Objects

We should avoid the use of sharp-edged objects, like needles, knives, blades, etc. These objects may cut our fingers and cause injury.

Fire

We should not play with lighted matchsticks or candles as they may cause burns to our body.

We should not light a matchstick near the gas stove. It may cause fire.

Some other Rules

We should not leave soap on the floor of the bathroom.

We may slip or fall.

We should not leave our toys on the floor of the room.

We should not run here and there in the house.

It can cause an accident.

We should throw the peels of fruits and vegetables into the dustbin. Peels lying on the floor can make someone slip and hurt.

Medicines

We should not touch or swallow any medicines without the permission of our parents or elders.

Glass Objects

We should not play with glasses, bowls or plates made of glass. If they fall, they might break into sharp pieces and cut our hands or feet.

Safety Rules in the Playground

We should not push others while playing.

We should wait for our turn while going to a swing or seesaw.

We should leave the park before it is dark.

We should throw the garbage into the dustbin, when we eat or drink something in the park.

Keep away from thorny plants and barbed wires.

Brainy Point

Remember, it is better to be safe than sorry.

Safety Rules on the Road

Always walk on the footpath.

Cross the road at the zebra crossing.

Wait for the traffic light to be green.

If the zebra crossing is not there, look to the right and then look to the left. Now, cross the road if the road is clear.

Never run across the road.

Do not block the road. Give way to others. Do not tease the street dog; it may also harm you.

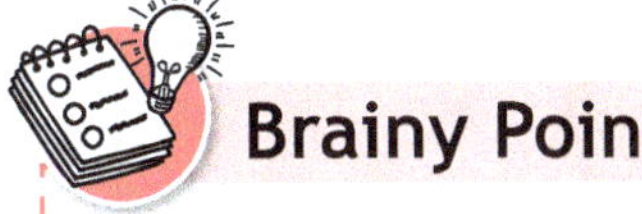

Brainy Point

The zebra crossing is also known as the pedestrian crossing.

Safety Rules While Riding the Bus

We should stand in a queue to get into the bus.

We should not get into or down a moving bus.

We should never lean out of the windows.

We should not disturb the driver. It may cause an accident.

Safety Rules While Boating and Swimming

We should travel in the boat carefully.

We should be seated at one place. We should not jump around.

We should not go swimming alone. We should use our swimming tube.

Safety Rules While Celebrating Festivals

We should always play Holi with safe herbal colours.

On Diwali, we should light candles and diyas when some elder is with us.

When we are in a large crowd at a fair or at a place of worship, we should not leave the hands of our parents. We should not go anywhere on our own.

Summary of the Chapter

- Safety habits keep us safe.
- We should always walk on the footpath.
- We should use the zebra crossing to cross the road.

A.   Answer the following questions :

1.   Where should we walk on the road?

2.   Why should we not play with sharp-edged objects?

3. Why should we not leave our toys on the floor?

4. Which colours should we use to play Holi?

5. Why should we not speak loudly in the bus?

B. Write 'S' for safe actions and 'U' for unsafe actions :

1. Throwing a banana peel on the road
2. Playing with a lighted matchstick near the gas stove
3. Crossing the road at the zebra crossing
4. Keeping the toys in their proper places
5. Using a hammer to hit a nail in the wall, when you are alone

C. Correct the underlined words and rewrite the sentences :

1. We should play <u>on the road</u>.

2. We <u>should not swim</u> in the presence of an adult.

3. We <u>should keep</u> the toys on the floor.

4. We <u>should speak</u> loudly in the bus.

5. We should light candles <u>without</u> the help of <u>anyone</u>.

D. **Tick (✓) the correct answer :**

1. When we are on the road, we should ________________ .

   a. run to cross the road   ☐

   b. walk in the middle of the road   ☐

   c. follow traffic light signals   ☐

2. We should avoid playing with ________________ .

   a. sharp things   ☐

   b. a bat and ball   ☐

   c. dolls   ☐

3. When we are in the classroom, we should ________________ .

   a. jump on chairs and tables   ☐

   b. throw pieces of chalk at one another   ☐

   c. sit quietly and open our books   ☐

 **Get Hands-on Experience...**

Make a 'First Aid Box' to keep at home. Keep all the essential things such as, adhesive bandage, ointment, scissors, painkiller tablets, etc. in it nicely.

 **Hands-on Learning...**

If you are in a park or at a public place and you see someone hurt, report an adult so that first aid may be given to him.

4 Domestic Animals

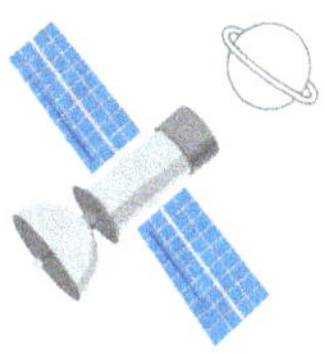

- **Domestic Animals**
- **Uses of Animals**
- **Pets**
- **Homes of Domestic Animals**

Rack Your Brain

Veena loves her pet dog and cat very much. But she wants to learn more about other animals. So, her parents took her to the zoo. In the zoo, Veena saw many animals. She was amazed and said, "Mom, all these animals are different from one another in so many ways." Mom replied, "Yes dear, all the animals have different features and different habits."

Dear children ! There is a great variety of animals all around us. They differ from one another. Let us know more about the different kinds of animals.

There are many animals around us. They live at different places and some of them are kept with us in our houses and fields.

Domestic Animals

The animals that are very useful to us and are kept at home as pets or on the farm are called domestic animals. We take special care of these animals. We provide them with food and shelter. They are useful in many ways.

Uses of Animals

Animals also give us many things like plants.

Milk

Some animals give us milk to drink.

Goat

Cow

Buffalo

Milk is very essential for good health. It is also used for making many things.

Butter

Curd

Cheese

Sweets

Eggs

Some animals give us eggs. Many people eat eggs.

Hen

Duck

Meat

Some animals give us flesh or meat. We cook their flesh to eat.

Fish

Prawn

Hen

Goat

Silk and Wool

We get silk from silkworms. Silken clothes are used in summers. They keep us cool. We get wool from a sheep's hair. Woollen clothes are used in winters. They keep us warm.

Silkworms   Silk saree   Sheep   Wool

Honey and Wax

We get honey and wax from beehives.

Beehive   Honey   Wax

Leather

The skins of dead animals like snakes, crocodiles, buffaloes, cows, camels and goats are used as leather. Leather is used for making bags, shoes, belts, jackets, suitcases, etc.

Crocodile   Leather Shoes   Bag   Suitcase   Snake

Manure and Fuel

The dung of some animals is dried and used as manure for plants and as fuel for burning. For example– cow, buffalo, horse and camel.

Beasts of Burden

Some animals are used for carrying loads for us such as horse, camel, ox, elephant, donkey, etc. The horse draws a cart called a tonga. The ox ploughs the field. The camel and the donkey carry loads. These animals work hard for us at farms.

Donkey

Elephant

Horse

Bullock

Brainy Point

The camel is called the "ship of the desert".

Pets

We keep cats, dogs, rabbits, parrots and pigeons as pets. Pets live with us as part of our family. We keep them for fun and safety. Dogs guard our homes from thieves. Cats keep rats away from our homes.

Cat

Dog

Pigeon

Parrot

Homes of Domestic Animals

Some animals live in the houses provided by us.

Cows in a shed

Horses in a stable

Sheep in a pen

Dog in a kennel

Hens in a coop

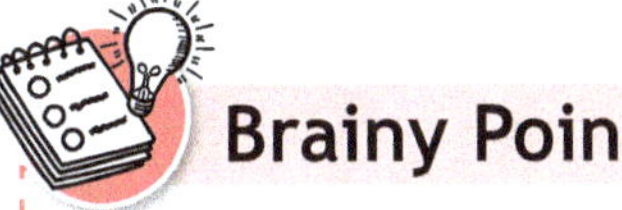

Brainy Point

A farm where cows are kept for getting milk is called a dairy farm.

Summary of the Chapter

- Animals are of different sizes, shapes and colours.
- We keep domestic animals at home as pets or on farms.
- Animals give us eggs, meat, honey, milk, wax, wool, leather and fuel.
- Animals carry heavy loads for us.

Let's Comprehend

A. Answer the following questions :

1. What are domestic animals?

2. From where do we get honey and wax?

3. Write the names of some milk products.

4. What do you mean by 'beasts of burden'?

5. How is the dung of some animals used?

____

6. Why is milk essential?

____

7. Why do we eat the flesh of animals?

____

B. Fill in the blanks with the suitable words :

1. Animals are ____________ in many ways.

2. Some animals give us ____________ to drink.

3. We get silk from ____________ .

4. The ____________ of dead animals is used for making leather.

5. The ____________ is called the 'ship of the desert'.

6. ____________ clothes are used in winters.

7. Silk clothes are used in ____________ .

C. Give two examples for each:

1. Milk ____________ ____________

2. Egg ____________ ____________

3. Meat ____________ ____________

4. Leather ____________ ____________

5. Beasts of burden ____________ ____________

6. Pet animals ____________ ____________

Get Hands-on Experience...

You pet dog is named 'BRUNO'. Enlist two ways in which you can take care of it.

____

____

Hands-on Learning...

A. Draw or paste the picture of an animal that you would like to tame at home in the given space:

B. Have you ever seen a beehive on a tree? You can see many bees sitting on a hive. They collect nectar sucked from the flowers to make honey in this hive. Honey tastes sweet and it is also a remedy for cough and cold.

5 Wild Animals

We Will Learn

- **Wild Animals**
- **Herbivorous Animals**
- **Carnivorous Animals**
- **Omnivorous Animals**
- **Scavengers**
- **Shelters of Wild Animals**

Rack Your Brain

Siana was very eager to see wild animals. She asked her Grandpa "Where do wild animals live ?" Grandpa said, "Wild animals actually live in the jungle. We cannot tame them. Now, we can keep them on the farm or at home. But you can see them in the zoo." On the weekend, Siana went for a visit to the zoo with her friends. At the zoo, she saw the animals in cages or roaming around freely in the enclosures. It was great fun!

In this chapter, we will learn about the different types of wild animals and their food and shelters.

Wild Animals

The animals that live in a jungle freely are called wild animals. Wild animals live in their natural surroundings. They roam about in search of food and shelter. They cannot be tamed.

Food of Wild Animals

Different wild animals eat different kinds of foods. We can divide wild animals into four groups on the basis of their eating habits.

Herbivorous Animals

The animals that eat only plants are called plant-eating animals or herbivorous animals.

Zebra

Elephant

Giraffe

Deer

Carnivorous Animals

The animals that hunt and eat the flesh of the other animals are called flesh-eating animals or carnivorous animals.

Tiger

Lion

Hawk

Crocodile

Omnivorous Animals

The animals that eat both plants and flesh are called omnivorous animals.

Crow

Bear

Scavengers

The animals that eat the flesh of dead animals are called scavengers. These animals help keep the forest clean.

Vulture

Hyena

Hawk

Dingo

Shelters of Wild Animals

All animals need homes or shelters to live in and to protect themselves from rain, cold, heat and enemies.

Some animals make homes for themselves

Animals like rats, moles and mongooses dig holes in the ground. Birds build their nests on the branches of trees.

Rat

Mongoose

Bird (nest)

Some animals live in the houses made by others

Rabbits live in burrows dug by other animals.

Snakes live in holes and ant-hills (holes dug by ants).

Rabbit (burrow)

Snake (hole)

Ant-hill

Some animals do not make their homes. They search for some safe places and start to live there. Bears live in caves. Lions and tigers live in dens. Monkeys and squirrels live on treetops.

Bear

Lion

Monkey

Squirrel

Some wild animals do not live in homes. They roam about in the jungle. Elephants, giraffes, zebras and deer seek shelter under huge trees. Gorillas live in open places in the forest.

Elephant

Deer

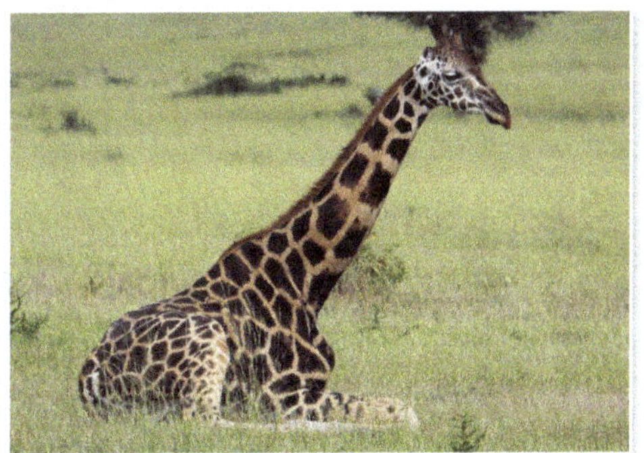
Giraffe

Some animals like fish, whale, etc. live in water only. Frogs, tortoises and crocodiles live both in water and on land.

Fish

Whale

Frog

Tortoise

Crocodile

Summary of the Chapter

- Animals living in jungles are called wild animals; they cannot be tamed.
- Wild animals eat plants, animals or both.
- Wild animals live under or on trees.

Let's Comprehend

A. Answer the following questions :

1. What are wild animals?

2. What do you mean by herbivorous animals?

3. What do you mean by omnivorous animals?

4. What is the difference between scavengers and carnivorous animals?

5. How do scavengers keep the forest clean?

B. Fill in the blanks using the suitable words :

1. Wild animals live in a ____________ freely.

2. Plant-eating animals are called ____________ animals.

3. Some animals make ____________ for themselves.

4. ____________ build their nests.

5. ____________ lives in open places in forests.

C. Give two examples for each :

1. Herbivorous animals

2. Carnivorous animals

3. Omnivorous animals

4. Scavengers

Get Hands-on Experience...

Do you think that we should take care of all animals ? We should never harm or hurt them in anyway. Discuss with your friends.

Hands-on Learning...

Stick the picture of your favourite wild animal in the given space and write its name:

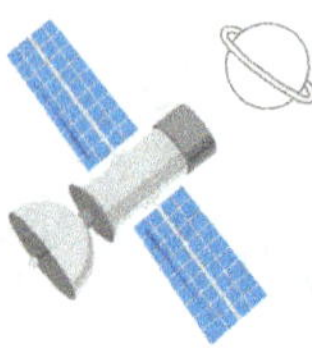

6 Different Kinds of Plants

We Will Learn

- **Different Kinds of Plants**
- **Water Plants**

Rack Your Brain

One day, Mrs Joshi took Siya and Aradhaya for a walk to the Botanical Garden. She asked the children to observe the plants around them. The children were very happy to see the plants. They observed that some plants are small and weak and some are big and tall. They also observed that plants look so different from one another. Do you also observe the sizes and shapes of plants around you? Are you a plant-lover? Do you grow and take care of plants outside your house? Dear children! We all should grow more and more plants as they are helpful in many ways. Let us learn more about the different types of plants.

Different Kinds of Plants

On the basis of the sizes, we can divide plants into many groups.

Trees

Trees are tall and strong plants. They can stand straight on the ground. They have thick, hard and woody stems called trunks. Most trees have branches. Trees live for many years.

Mango Tree

Pine Tree

Banyan Tree

Peepal Tree

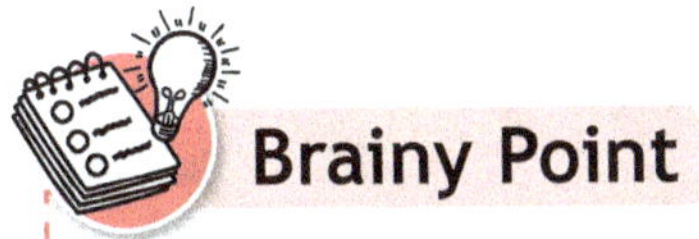

Brainy Point

The little plant that grows out of a seed is called a seedling.

Shrubs

Shrubs are bushy plants. They are smaller than trees. They have many thin and woody stems rising from the ground. These branches are very closely knitted, so they look bushy. Some of these plants have thorns. Shrubs live for a few years only.

Rose

Mehndi

China Rose

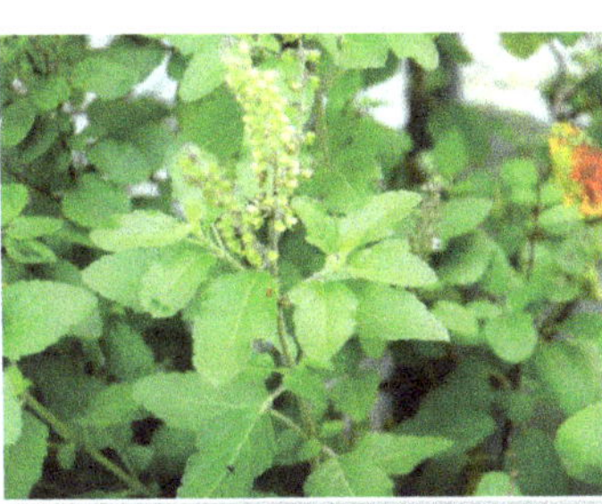

Tulsi

Herbs

Herbs are very small plants. They have thin and non-woody stems. Their stems are green in colour. Many herbs live just for one season. Within one season, they grow into their full sizes, produce flowers and fruits.

Mint

Maize

Spinach

Grass

Brainy Point

The banana plant is tall, but it is a herb because it has a soft stem.

Climbers

Climbers have weak stems, so they cannot stand erect. They need support to stand. They climb with the help of fences, walls and sticks. Some climbers like pea live only for one season only. Others like money plant can live for many years.

Grapevine

Money Plant

Pea Plant

Cucumber

Brainy Point

Over 130 plant families include climbers.

Creepers

Creepers have very weak stems. They creep along the ground. They never stand upright.

Pumpkin

Watermelon

Strawberries

Sweet Potatoes

Water Plants

The plants that grow in water are called water plants. Most water plants are herbs.

Lotus

Hydrilla

Water Hyacinth

Duckweed

Brainy Point

The most common colour variations of the lotus flower are pink and white.

Summary of the Chapter

- Trees are big and tall with strong trunks.
- Shrubs are small and bushy with woody stems.
- Herbs have soft and green stems.
- The plants that grow in water are called water plants.

Let's Comprehend

A. **Answer the following questions :**

1. Write two lines on trees.

2. How is the stem of a creeper different from the stem of a tree?

3. Why do climbers need support to stand?

4. The banana plant is tall but it is a herb. Why?

B. **Fill in the blanks with the suitable words :**

1. ______________ have hard stems.

2. Some shrubs have ____________.

3. The banana plant is an example of a ____________.

4. ____________ cannot stand erect.

5. Most ____________ plants are herbs.

6. The little plant grows out of a seed is called a ____________ .

C. Tick (✓) the correct answer :

1. These plants live for many years ____________ .

   a. Trees ☐   b. Shrubs ☐   c. Herbs ☐

2. These plants grow in water ____________ .

   a. Herbs ☐   b. Climbers ☐   c. Water Plants ☐

3. They creep along the ground ____________ .

   a. Climbers ☐   b. Herbs ☐   c. Creepers ☐

4. These plants live only for one season ____________ .

   a. Climbers ☐   b. Herbs ☐   c. Creepers ☐

5. These plants can stand straight on the ground ____________ .

   a. Trees ☐   b. Creepers ☐   c. Shrubs ☐

D. Match the following :

Column A	Column B
1. Trees	a. Non-woody stems
2. Climbers	b. Thin woody stems
3. Herbs	c. Weak stems
4. Shrubs	d. Thick, hard, woody stems

Get Hands-on Experience...

Make a list of at least ten different types of plants that you find in your surroundings.

Hands-on Learning...

Draw a plant you would like to grow in your house. Write its name:

7 Useful Plants

We Will Learn

- **Food From Plants**
- **Other Products From Plants**

Rack Your Brain

Tom was sitting with his mother on the dining table. He was very happy to see his favourite fruits and vegetables and lots of foodgrains too. He asked his mother, "Where does all this food come from ?" Mother replied, "We get almost all our food from plants." Plants give us not only fruits and vegetables but also other useful things.

So, we can say that plants are our green friends. Without them our life is not possible. In this chapter, we will learn about the products we get from plants and their uses.

Food from Plants

Plants make their own food with the help of air, water and Sunlight. They store it in different parts such as roots, stems, leaves, flowers and fruits.

Cereals and Pulses

Plants give us most of our food. We eat the various parts of plants. Cereals and pulses are seeds. They are the essential part of our food.

Wheat

Rice

Corn

Gram

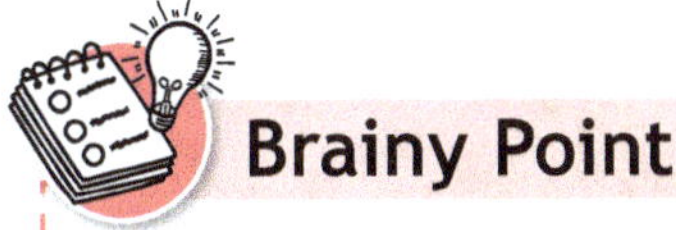

Brainy Point

We should wash fruits and vegetables before eating them.

Vegetables

The stems, leaves, roots and the fruits of plants are eaten as vegetables.

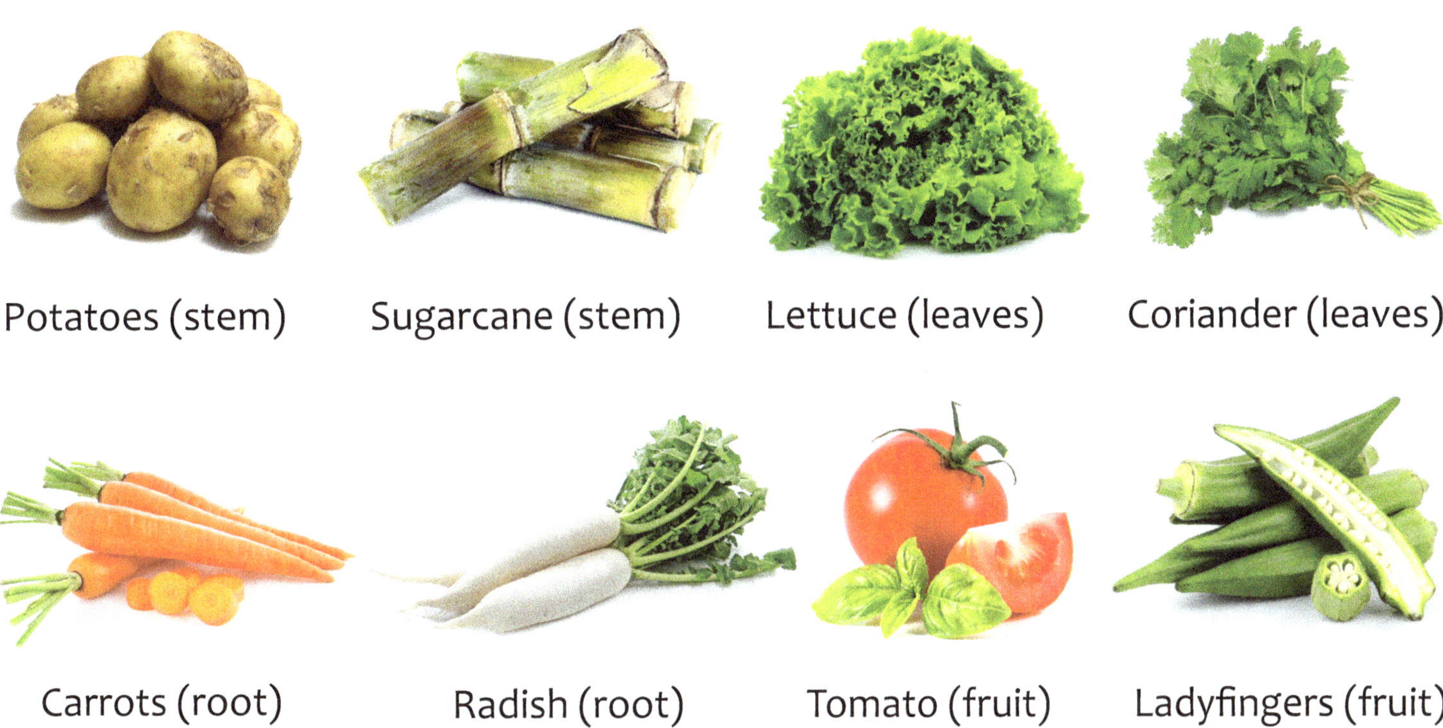

Potatoes (stem) Sugarcane (stem) Lettuce (leaves) Coriander (leaves)

Carrots (root) Radish (root) Tomato (fruit) Ladyfingers (fruit)

Fruits

Plants give us fleshy, juicy fruits and dried fruits.

Mangoes Apple Grapes Pineapple

Fleshy Fruits **Juicy Fruits**

Coconut

Walnut

Dried Fruits

Brainy Point

We should eat one fruit daily to stay healthy.

Oil

We get cooking oil from groundnuts, coconuts and from mustard and Sunflower seeds. We crush the seeds to get oil. Oil is also used for making soaps.

Mustard oil

Coconut oil

Sunflower oil

Drinks (cocoa, tea and coffee)

We get tea, coffee and cocoa from plants.

Cocoa beans, tea leaves and coffee beans are used for drinks. Cocoa beans are used for making chocolate and Coca Cola as well.

Cocoa Beans

Chocolate

Tea leaves

Tea

Coffee plant

Coffee

Other Products From Plants

Wood

We get wood from tree-trunks. Things like doors, windows, chairs, tables are made from sal, teak and rosewood. Pencils are also made from wood. Wood is used as fuel in villages.

Pencil

Firewood

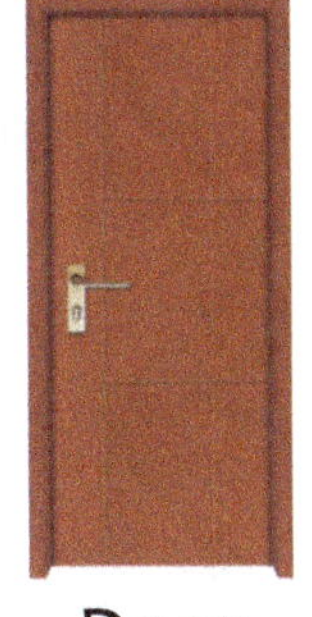

Door

Chair

Fibres

We get fibres such as jute, coconut and cotton. Cotton yields fibres for clothes. Jute and coconut yield fibres to make sacks, ropes and mats.

Cotton plant

Cotton dress

Jute

Jute bag

Coconut tree

Medicines

Some plants like neem, poppy, aloe vera, mint, garlic, eucalyptus, tulsi, etc. are used for making medicines.

Neem

Poppies

Eucalyptus

Aloe Vera

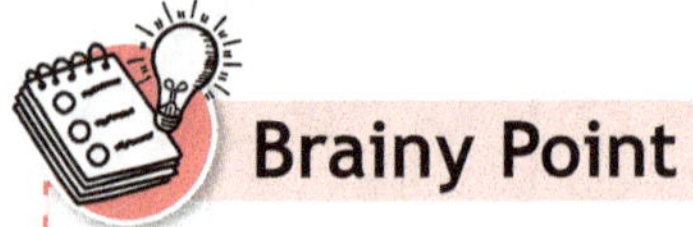

Brainy Point

Aloe vera juice is very beneficial in stomach aches for kids.

Paper, Gum and Rubber

The wood of some plants such as bamboo and pine is used for making paper. Gum is made from the juice of the acacia stem. Rubber is made from the white milk of the rubber tree.

Bamboo   Paper   Acacia   Gum   Rubber tree   Tyre

Decoration, Colours, Scents and Perfumes

We decorate our homes with flowers and leaves. We get colour from the flowers and leaves of some plants. These colours are used for painting and dyeing. Scents and perfumes are made from flowers like rose and jasmine.

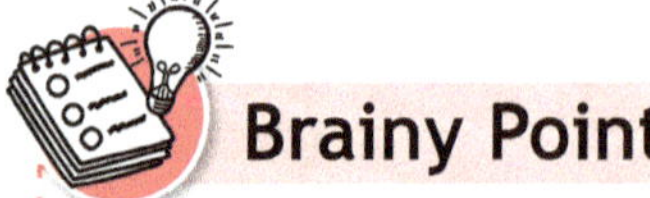

Brainy Point

Plants provide shade, shelter and home to many birds and animals.

Rose   Champa   Jasmine   Phlox

Big trees give us shade on a hot, Sunny day. Thorny plants are used as hedges.

Fodder and Manure

Animals eat the grasses, leaves and branches of plants. The waste part of plants is used as manure. And all the more, plants make the air fresh and clean. And we breathe in air.

Summary of the Chapter

- Plants are very useful to us.
- We eat the different parts of a plant.
- Plants give us food, oil, drinks and medicines.
- Paper, gum, rubber and scents are made from plants.

Let's Comprehend

A.   Answer the following questions :

1.   What three things do plants need to make their food?

2.   Where do plants store food?

3.   Name three plants that are used for making medicines.

4.   Which plant is used for making gum?

5.   What do plants give us?

6.   Which plants are helpful in making paper?

B. **Fill in the blanks using the suitable words :**

1. Cereals and pulses are _______________ .

2. Lettuce is an example of the _______________ of a plant.

3. We _______________ seeds to get oil.

4. Wood is used as _______________ in villages.

5. The cotton plant yields _______________ for clothes.

6. We get _______________ from tree-trunks.

C. **Give two examples for each :**

1. Roots _______________ _______________

2. Stems _______________ _______________

3. Leaves _______________ _______________

4. Fruits _______________ _______________

5. Flowers _______________ _______________

6. Medicines _______________ _______________

D. **Which part of each of the following plants is used as food ?**

1. Sugar cane _______________

2. Cabbage _______________

3. Carrot _______________

4. Radish _______________

5. Wheat _______________

6. Pea _______________

7. Mango _______________

8. Lettuce _______________

Get Hands-on Experience...

Ask your mom to cut some fruits in small pieces and make fruit salad. Sprinkle chat masala on it and enjoy the healthy dish:

Hands-on Learning...

Draw your favourite fruit and vegetable and colour them beautifully:

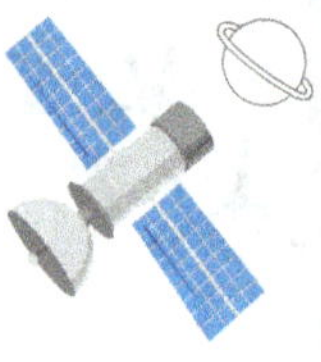

8   Air

We Will Learn

- What Does Air Contain?
- Wind
- Breeze
- Gale
- Storm
- Properties of Air
- Breathe Fresh and Clean Air

Rack Your Brain

Dear Children ! Have you ever seen air? Certainly not. No one can see air. But we can feel air when it moves. When we switch on a fan and sit in front of it, we feel air touching our body. All living beings need air to breathe. We cannot live without air. Let us read more about it in detail.

What Does Air Contain?

Air is a mixture of many gases. It also contains many other things. Some of the things are– water vapour, smoke, dust particles, germs.

Water vapour

When we put wet clothes in the Sun, the clothes become dry after some time. Where does the water go from clothes? The water goes into the air. Thus, the air contains this water as water vapour.

Smoke

Smoke coming out from factories, homes, cars, buses and trucks mixes with the air.

Dust Particles

When sweepers sweep floors, dust rises up into the air. Dust also mixes with the air when wind blows.

Germs

When a sick man coughs, germs from his cough go into the air. The air containing germs causes diseases.

Smoke, dust particles and germs make the air impure.

Wind

Moving air is called wind. We can't see it but we can see things moving in the wind. Wind helps us in many ways.

Wind moves a sailboat.

Wind turns the blades of a windmill.

Wind dries our wet clothes.

Wind helps hot-air balloons to fly.

Wind also carries the seeds of some plants away to new places.

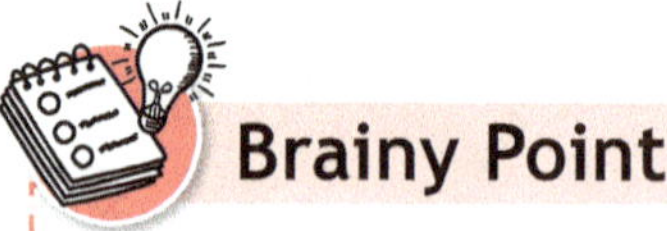

Brainy Point

Wind brings about the rainy weather.

Breeze

A gentle blowing wind is known as a breeze. The leaves of a tree rustle when a breeze blows.

Gale

A strong wind is called a gale. Gales can blow off the branches of trees.

Storm

Very strong winds are called storms. They are harmful. They are so strong that they break off the branches of trees or even uproot big trees. They can also blow away huts and houses. They can knock down electric poles. They can also sink/damage boats and ships.

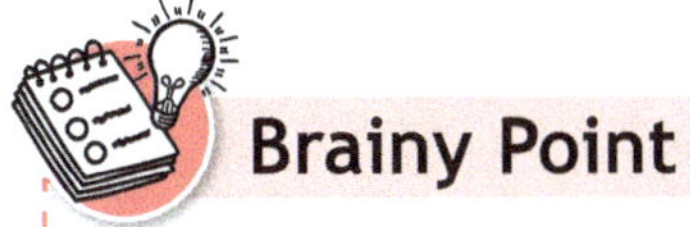

Impure air harms our lungs. It can cause diseases like asthma and TB.

Properties of Air

Air occupies The Space

Air occupies the space. When we blow air into a balloon, it fills the space inside the balloon. Filled air gives shape to the balloon.

Air has Weight

When we compare an air-filled balloon with the deflated one, we find that the inflated balloon is heavier than the deflated one.

Breathe Fresh and Clean Air

We must breathe in clean and fresh air to keep ourselves healthy. We should always play in the open field.

We should keep windows open to let fresh air in the house. We should not cover our faces when we sleep.

We can keep the air fresh and clean by

a. planting trees
b. walking or using a bicycle instead of other vehicles that produce smoke.

- Air is all around us.
- We can feel air but cannot see it.
- The air that has dust, smoke and germs is bad for us to breathe.
- We need fresh and clean air to keep us healthy.

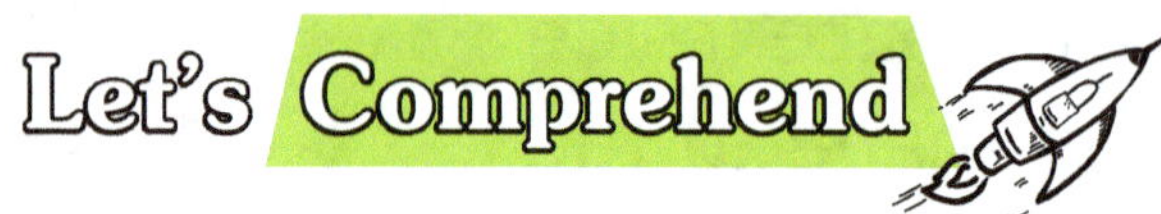

Let's Comprehend

A. Answer the following questions :

1. What is wind? How is it useful to us?

2. What does the air contain?

3. From where does the air get dust?

4. How does the air get impure?

5. What happens when we breathe in impure air?

B. Fill in the blanks using the suitable words :

1. ________________ is a mixture of many gases.

2. The water from wet clothes goes into the ____________ .

3. Wind turns the ____________ of a windmill.

4. A strong wind is called a ____________ .

5. Air ____________ the space.

C. **Match the following :**

Column A		Column B
1. breeze		a. fast and strong
2. storm		b. moving air
3. seeds		c. gentle and soft
4. wind		d. water vapour
5. water from clothes		e. carried to other places

D. **Name the following :**

1. Two things that air contain.

   ___________________   ___________________

2. Two names of blowing air.

   ___________________   ___________________

E. **Tick (✓) the correct answer :**

1. Dust and smoke make the air ___________.

   a. fresh ☐   b. dirty ☐   c. clean ☐

2. We must breathe in ___________.

   a. clean air ☐   b. smoke ☐   c. water vapour ☐

3. Plants make the air ___________.

   a. dirty ☐   b. polluted ☐   c. clean ☐

4. Very strong moving air causes a ___________.

   a. wind ☐   b. breeze ☐   c. storm ☐

Get Hands-on Experience...

Let's see how air moves things.

Take a long ribbon. Let it hang free under a stack of books on a table. Make sure the table is placed under a fan.

Switch on the fan at its lowest speed.

Observe the ribbon (Tick the correct choice)

- How does the ribbon move?
  Fast/Slow
- Now, increase the speed of the fan.
  Observe the ribbon.
- How does the ribbon move now?
  Fast/Slow.

Hands-on Learning...

Take some soap solution in a mug. Dip a straw in it. Take out the straw and blow air into it. Observe the bubbles floating in the air.

9 Forms of Water

- Sources of Water
- Drink Clean Water
- Storage of Drinking Water
- How does Water Get Dirty?
- Save Water
- Forms of Water

Rack Your Brain

One day, the science teacher Mrs Mehta asked the students, "Have you seen your mom filling up the ice-tray with water and keeping it in the freezer ? What happens to the water after some time ?"

Siena said, "It becomes ice." Mrs Mehta asked , "What happens if the tray with ice cubes is left outside on the table ?"

"It becomes water," answered the students in one voice.

In this chapter, you will learn about water and its three forms.

Sources of Water

We get water from many sources. Rain is the main source of water. Rainwater gets collected in rivers, ponds, lakes, streams and springs.

Rain

River

Lake

Some rainwater goes deep inside the earth. This is called ground water. We dig wells, tubewells and handpumps to get this underground water.

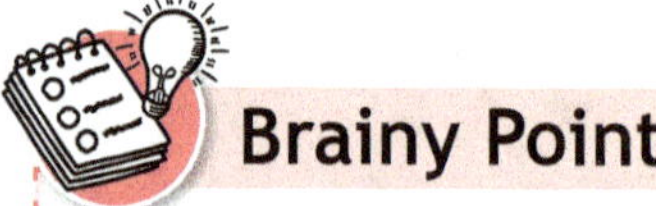

Brainy Point

Around sixty-six per cent of the human body is made up of water.

Well

Handpump

Drink Clean Water

Water may not always be clean. Dirty water contains germs. Drinking dirty water can make us feel sick. We need to drink clean water.

There are two methods to make water safe for drinking.

- **Boiling** - Boiling water for about 20 minutes kills germs.
  After cooling, the boiled water becomes fit for drinking and cooking.
- **Using water filters** - In houses, we can get clean water by using filters.

Boiling

Filtering

Storage of Drinking Water

Storage of water means collecting water for future use. Water can be stored in tanks, tubs and buckets.

We should always use a clean container to store water. We should also keep it covered.

How Does Water Get Dirty?

Water from ponds, lakes and rivers gets dirty when people wash clothes in rivers or animals bathe in them.

Using dirty water is not good for health. You can help to keep water clean.

  Never throw waste things into ponds, rivers, lakes and seas.

  Plant lots of trees around water bodies.

Save Water

Water is present all around us, but very little of it is safe to drink. So, we must use this water very carefully. We should not waste water.

Ways for Saving Water

The water we get from taps is very precious. Most of the water present on the earth is sea water, which is salty and cannot be used by us. Only water from ponds, lakes, streams, rivers and rainwater collected in huge tanks or underground can be used. The useful water present on the earth is very less for the large number of people and animals living on the earth. Therefore, we should not waste water. We should follow the given points for saving water.

- We should take water in a bucket for bathing. It will waste less water than a shower.
- Taps should be turned off when not in use.
- Close the tap tightly after use.
- If the tap is leaking, get it repaired soon.
- Do not keep the tap running while brushing your teeth or rubbing your hands with soap.

Forms of Water

Water is found in three forms:-solid, liquid and gas.

The water itself is in liquid form. We cannot hold water because it flows away.

When the water is cooled, it changes into ice. Ice is the solid form of water.

When the water is heated, it changes into (steam) vapour. Vapour is the gaseous form of water.

Liquid

Solid

Gas

Brainy Point

Water is the only substance on the earth that is naturally present in all three different forms.

Summary of the Chapter

- All living things need water.
- We use water every day for many things.
- We get water from rivers, ponds and lakes.
- Water has three forms : solid, liquid and gas.

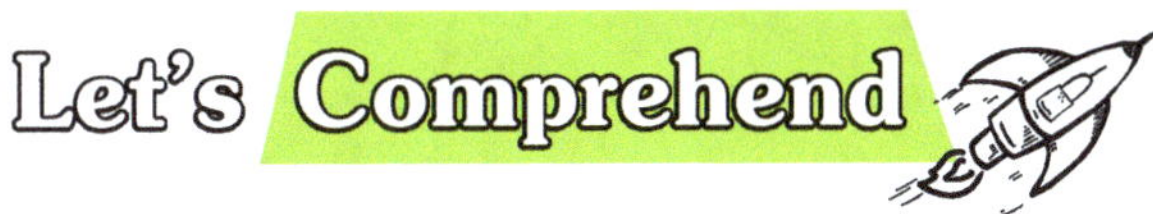

A. Answer the following questions :

1. How do we get the underground water?

2. Write two methods to make water safe for drinking.

3. Why can we not use the sea water for drinking?

4. Write three ways for saving water.

5. What are the three forms of water?

6. Does water have its own colour, taste and odour?

B. Fill in the blanks with the suitable words :

1. ___________ is the main source of water.

2. Dirty water contains ___________.

3. We can get clean water by using the ___________.

4. We should keep the drinking water ___________.

5. We should not ___________ water.

6. Water itself is in ___________ form.

C. Write 'T' for a true statement and 'F' for a false one :

1. The main sources of water are rivers and ponds.

2. Drinking dirty water can make us feel sick.

3. Steam is the gaseous form of water.

4. We should take a shower while bathing.

D. Tick (✓) the correct option :

1. In the solid form, water is (water vapour / ice).

2. Water vapour or steam is (solid / gas).

3. Boiling water changes into (water vapour / ice).

4. Water has (four / three) different forms.

5. Water in (liquid / gaseous) form is not visible to us.

Get Hands-on Experience...

We need water for many activities. Here, some uses are given; draw the pictures for them :

drinking

bathing

watering plants

cleaning

washing

Hands-on Learning...

Make a paper boat. Try to sail the boat in a rain puddle.

10 Housing and Clothing for Us

- Different Types of Houses
- Different Types of Roofs
- Need for Clothes
- Types of Clothes

Rack Your Brain

Dear children ! Observe your surroundings carefully. There are many kinds of houses around you. Houses protect us from rain, heat and cold. They also protect us from thieves and dangerous animals. Similarly, clothes are also one of our basic needs. They protect our body from heat, cold, wind, rain and dust. They also make us look smart. Now, let us discuss them in detail.

Different Types of Houses

People make different types of houses using different materials.

Pucca House

These houses are built of bricks, cement, sand and steel. Doors and windows are made of wood and glass. These houses are strong and last for a long time. Nowadays, most of the houses in the cities are pucca houses.

Pucca House

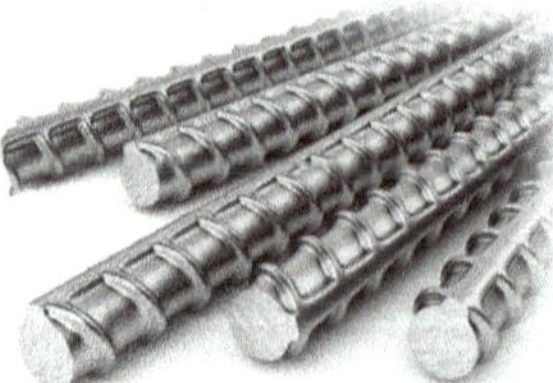

Materials

The following are the different types of permanent houses.

Cottage

Bungalow

Apartment

Kutcha House

These houses are made of mud, straw, grass, bamboo, etc. These are small houses. These houses are not very strong.

Kutcha House

Materials

Kutcha houses are mainly found in villages.

Kutcha houses are also called temporary houses because they do not last very long. The following are some other examples of temporary houses.

Totally wooden
house (on hills)

Wood and bamboo
house (on hills)

Straw and mud house
(in plains)

Igloos

When the Eskimos go hunting, they build igloos for shelter. Igloos are houses made up of ice blocks.

Moveable Houses

The houses that can be moved from one place to another are called moveable houses. The people who have to move from place to place for their work, make moveable houses. For example– Tent, Caravan, Houseboat.

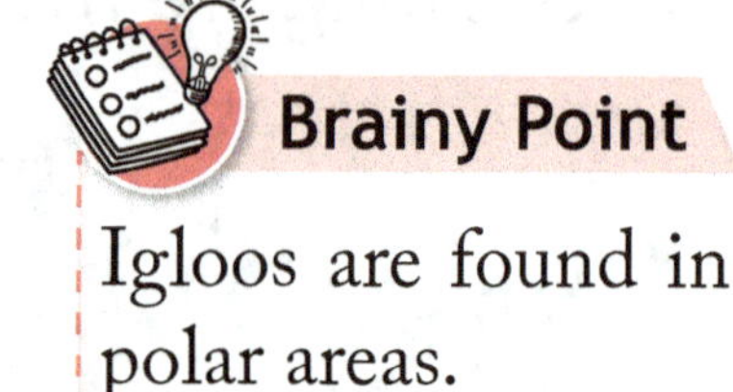

Igloos are found in polar areas.

Tent

Caravan

Houseboat

Different Types of Roofs

The roof is the topmost part of a house. Houses have different kinds of roofs.

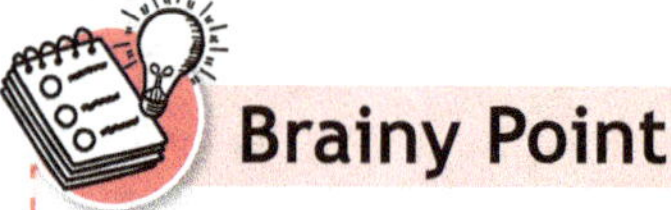

The caravan is used by the gypsies.

Flat Roofs

The houses in the plains have flat roofs. These are made of steel bars, cement and bricks.

Flat Roof

Sloping roof

Sloping Roofs

The houses in the hills have sloping roofs. These roofs help rainwater or snow to slide off easily.

Semi-Circular Roofs

Snow houses or igloos have semi-circular roofs. Many subways have also semi-circular roofs.

Need for Clothes

We all need to wear clothes to protect ourselves from heat, cold, wind and rain.

They also make us look smart.

Subway

Types of Clothes

We wear different types of clothes in different seasons.

Shirt

Knickers

Frock

We wear thin cotton clothes in the summer season. Cotton clothes keep our body cool in the hot weather. We wear woollen clothes in the winter season. Woollen clothes keep our body warm in the biting cold.

Sweater

Cap

Muffler

When it rains, we wear raincoats and gumboots and carry umbrellas to keep ourselves dry.

Raincoat

Gumboots

Umbrella

Brainy Point

Fibres from hundreds of cocoons are used for making one small silk scarf.

Summary of the Chapter

- Houses are the places where we live with our families.
- Houses protect us from rain, heat, cold and thieves.
- Clothes protect our body from heat, cold, wind, rain and dust.
- We wear different types of clothes in different seasons.

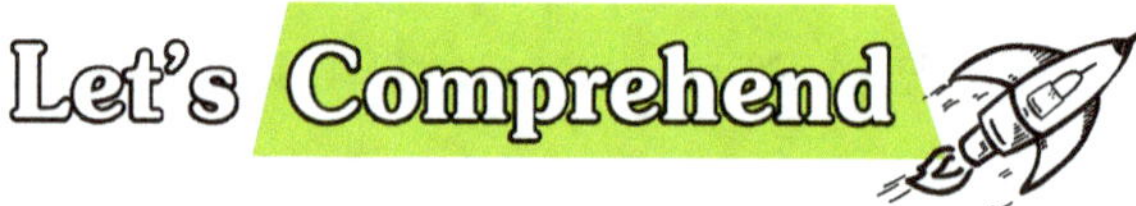

A. **Answer the following questions :**

1. Why does each of us need a house?

2. Mention any two differences between permanent houses and temporary houses.

3. Why are the houses in the hills built with sloping roofs?

   ____

4. Why do we wear raincoats and gumboots in the rainy season?

   ____

B. **Fill in the blanks with suitable words :**

1. We all feel _____________ and _____________ in our houses.

2. Pucca houses are called _____________ houses.

3. Kutcha houses are called _____________ houses.

4. _____________ is used by the gypsies.

5. We should always wear _____________ clothes.

C. **There are some words related to the different types of houses; search for them and write in the given space :**

C	Q	G	U	K	L	T	E	N	T
A	R	Q	H	U	T	N	V	Q	C
R	F	L	A	T	R	B	W	T	O
A	S	P	U	C	C	A	S	U	T
V	U	R	W	H	W	M	N	M	T
A	R	S	O	A	R	B	O	N	A
N	N	I	G	L	O	O	P	R	G
B	U	N	G	A	L	O	W	F	E
T	A	P	A	R	T	M	E	N	T

____

____

____

____

____

____

____

1. House made of snow
2. Moveable House
3. Permanent House
4. Temporary House

Get Hands-on Experience...

Collect your old and discarded clothes and donate them to the people who don't have clothes. How do you feel after that?

Hands-on Learning...

Make designs on the dresses to make them look beautiful:

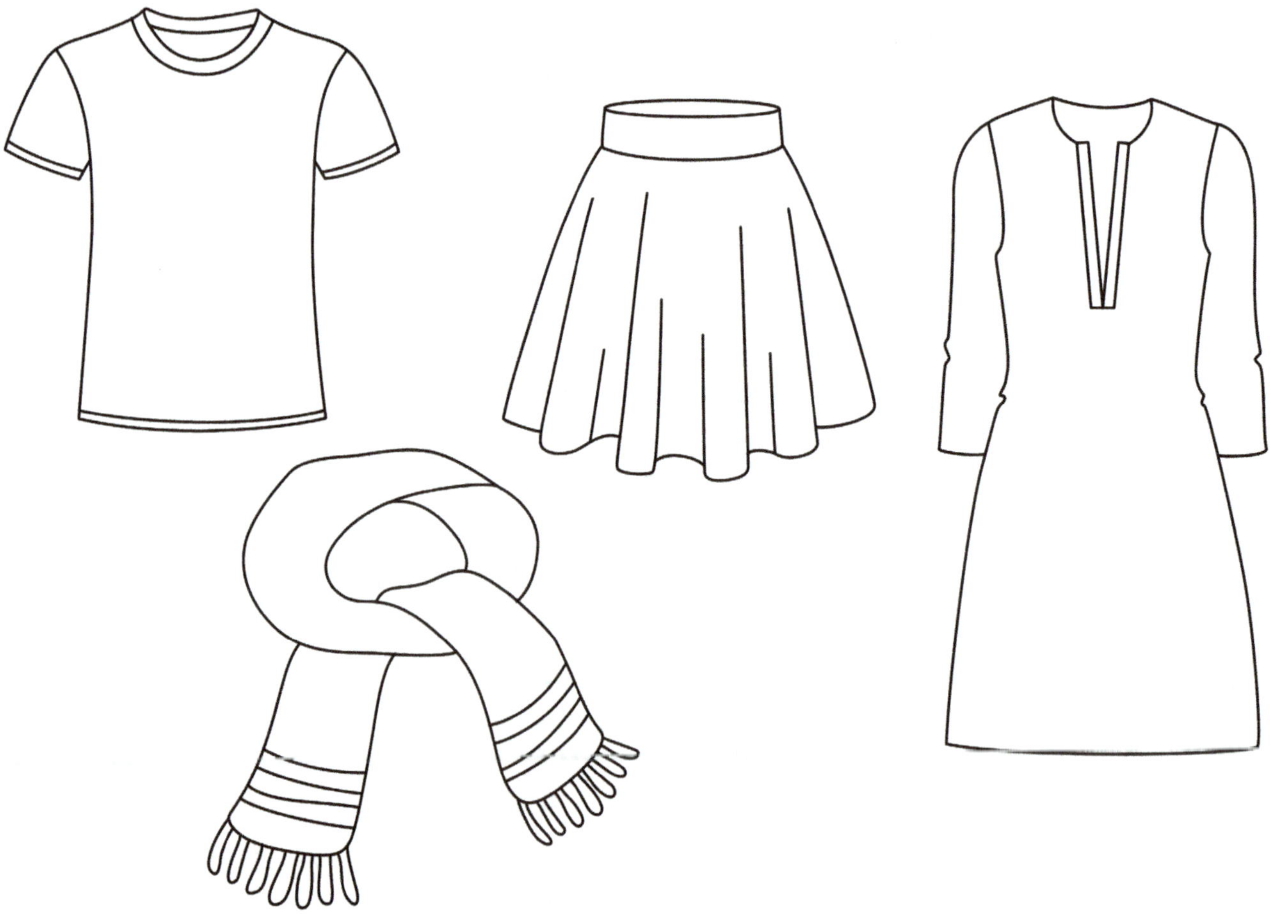

11 Rocks and Minerals

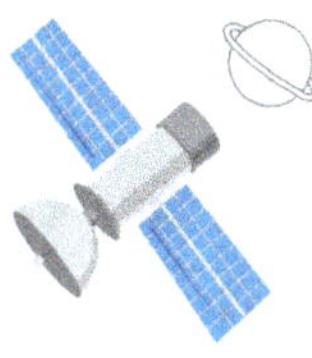

We Will Learn

- Rocks
- Hard Rocks
- Soft Rocks
- Uses of Rocks
- Minerals

 **Rack Your Brain**

Vijay, Sanjay and Jaya are friends. One fine day, they went trekking to the mountains. They saw big and small stones of different colours and shapes. Jaya started collecting them in her bag. Next day, when they met in the school, Jaya showed the stones. She asked the teacher, "Where do these stones come from and why are they so different from one another ?" The teacher told them that the stones come from the rocks.

Children ! The earth on which we live is mostly made up of rocks. Let us learn more about rocks.

Rocks

Rocks are found everywhere, on and under the earth. Mountains are made of rocks and rocks are also found near rivers and seas.

Rocks can be of different colours, shapes and sizes. Some rocks are rough to touch while some are smooth.

Rocks are of different colours like brown, white, black, green and red.

Rocks break down to form stones.

They break down due to the action of the wind, rain, cold and heat of the Sun.

There are many different kinds of rocks on the earth. Let us study more about them.

Hard Rocks

Granite is a very hard rock. It is found in white, pink or light grey colour. It is polished smooth and then used for making floor tiles, kitcken shelves, walls of buildings and statues.

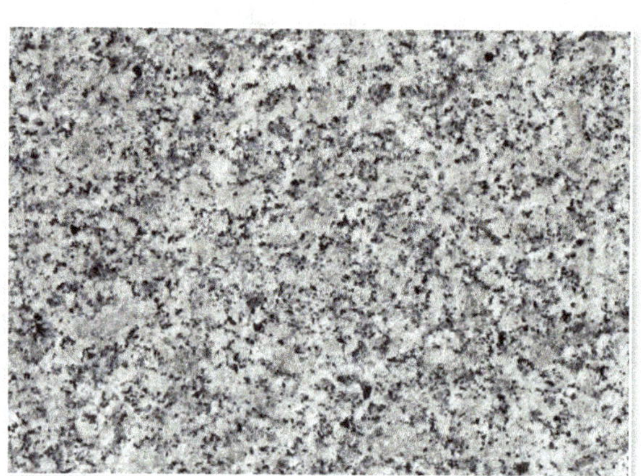

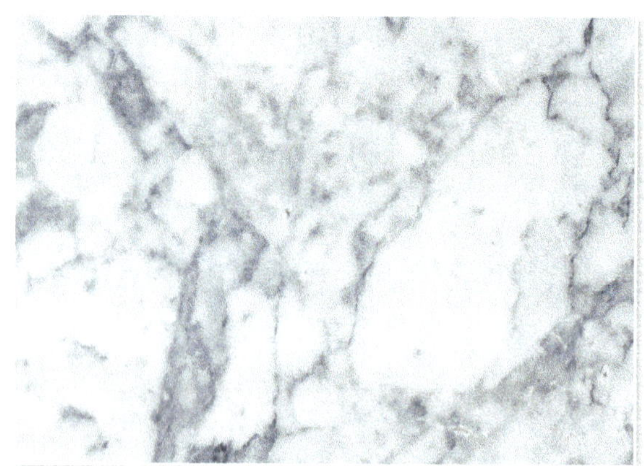

Marble is also a hard rock. It can be cut into small pieces. It is found in different colours and patterns.

It is used for making buildings, floors of houses, decorative items, etc.

Marble Rock

Taj Mahal

Made of Marble

Hawa Mahal

Sandstone is hard but softer than marble and granite. It is used for making buildings and statues.

Sandstone

Red Fort

Jama Masjid

Made of Red Sandstone

Soft Rocks

The rocks which can be broken easily are called soft rocks.

Coal is a soft rock. It is black in colour. It is used as fuel for cooking and running steam engines.

Slate is also a soft rock. Slate tiles are used as roofs for buildings. Slate is also used for making writing slates and blackboards.

Chalk is a very soft rock. It is easy to break. It is formed in different colours. It is used for writing on the blackboard. It is also used for making beautiful carvings.

Rocks have been used by humans for millions of years, from early tools and weapons to various construction materials.

Coal

Slate

Chalk

Uses of Rocks

Rocks are very useful to us. Here are some uses of rocks:

1. Rocks are used for making houses.
2. Rocks are used for making statues and decorative items.
3. Stones are used for making roads.
4. Stones are used for making a garden attractive.

Brainy Point

A scientist who studies rocks is called a geologist.

Minerals

All rocks are made up of menerals. Minerals are of different colours and sizes. They are used for making different things related to our daily life.

Different Minerals are used for different purposes.

Mercury is used in the thermometer.

Graphite is used for making pencil leads.

Diamond is the hardest mineral. It is used for making jewellery. It is also used for cutting glass.

Talc is used for making talcum powder. It is the softest mineral.

Quartz is used in watches.

Gemstones are hard and colourful minerals. They are cut into different shapes and then polished.

They are used for making jewellery. Ruby, emerald, corals are some examples of gemstones.

Brainy Point

The people who go inside mines to dig rocks are called miners.

Summary of the Chapter

- Rocks differ in sizes, shapes, hardness and colours.
- Rocks are used for making buildings, statues , floors, jewellery, etc.
- Rocks contain minerals.

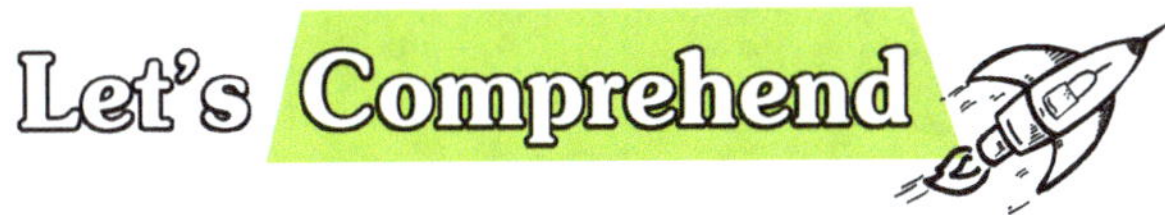

A. Answer the following questions :

1. Where can we find rocks on the earth?

2. How do rocks break down?

3. Write two lines about sandstone.

4. Which rock material is used for making roofs for buildings?

5. What are gemstones? Name any two gemstones.

 Fill in the blanks with the suitable words :

1. Our earth is made up of very big ___________ .

2. ___________ is a soft rock and easy to break.

3. ___________ are also made of rocks.

4. Granite is a very ___________ rock.

5. All rocks are made up of ___________ .

6. ___________ are used for making roads.

C. **Name the rock or mineral :**

1. It is used for making decorative items.

2. It is used for making jewellery.

3. It is used for cutting glass.

4. It is used as fuel.

5. It is used for writing on a blackboard.

6. It is used for making buildings.

7. It is used for running steam engines.

8. It is used for making talcum powder.

D. **Write 'T' for a true statement and 'F' for a false one :**

1. The Red Fort is made of white marble.

2. Rocks are of different shapes, sizes and colours.

3. Rocks are used for making buildings and statues.

4. Deep holes made to dig out rocks are called mines.

5. Sandstone is used for making chalk.

Get Hands-on Experience...

Visit a nearby temple. Observe idols and statues there. Observe the rocks they are made up of :

Hands-on Learning...

Make a paper weight out of a rock. Choose a stone with a flat base. Make it smooth by rubbing with a file. Decorate it with beads, colours and other things. Present it to your teacher:

12 The Sun and Shadows

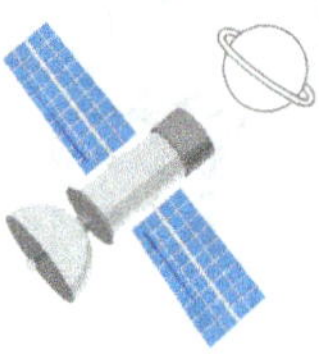

We Will Learn

- **The Sun**
- **What Happens When the Sun Rises?**
- **Finding the Directions**
- **Shadow**
- **Shadows Change Length and Direction**

Rack Your Brain

It was the morning time. Tom went out for a walk alone. He found that he was not alone. Someone was following him. It was dark and black in colour. When Tom ran, it also ran with him. When he stopped, it also stopped there.

Can you guess what it is? It is the shadow. Have you ever observed your shadow?

Let us study it.

The Sun

The Sun is a big ball of fire.

The Sun looks small because it is very away from the earth.

Even then, the Sun is the nearest star.

What Happens When the Sun Rises?

The Sun rises in the east.

As the Sun rises, the day begins.

The light of the Sun spreads all around on the earth.

The day becomes bright and warm. Flowers bloom in its light. Fruits ripen with its heat.

Green plants make their food in Sunlight.

The heat of the Sun provides us with vitamin D which is essential for our bones.

We work and play in daylight.

The Sun sets in the west and it becomes night. At night, there is darkness all around the earth. The night time becomes cool.

Finding the Directions

The direction in which the Sun rises in the morning is east. When we stand facing the rising Sun and stretch out our arms, our left hand points towards the north and our right hand points towards the south. Our back is towards the west.

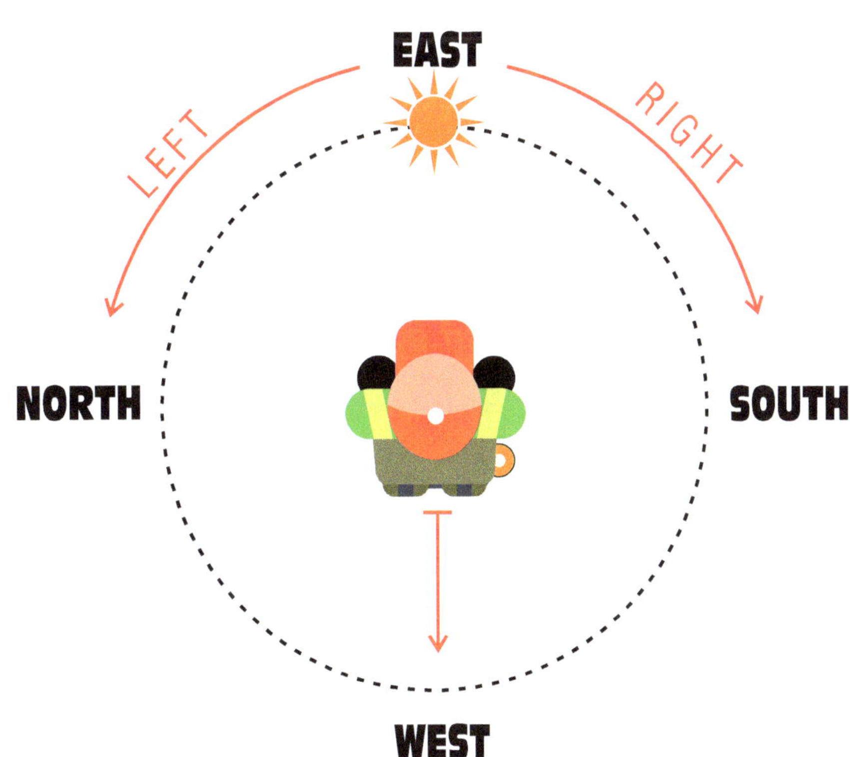

Shadow

The Sun gives us light. Light travels in a straight line.

When an object comes in the way of light, a shadow is formed.

When we walk or stand or sit under the Sun, our shadows are formed on the ground.

Shadows Change Length and Direction

Shadows are long in the morning and in the evening. Shadows are very short at noon when the Sun is overhead.

  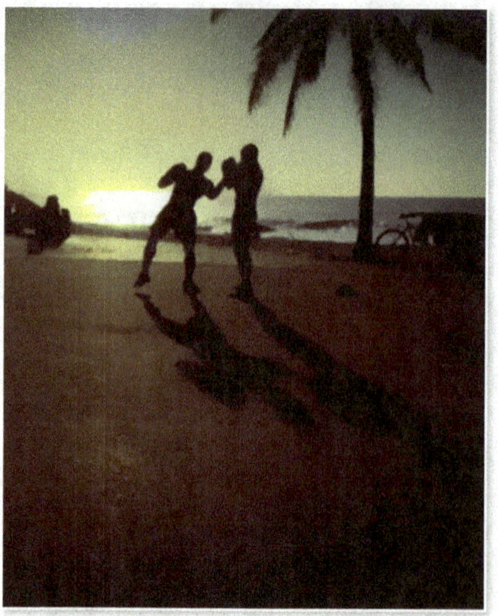

At night, shadows are formed by moonlight, candlelight or electric light.

Shadow is formed in the opposite direction to the source of light.

No shadow is formed in darkness when there is no light.

Brainy Point

The Sun is many times bigger than the moon. They both appear almost the same size because the Sun is very far from us.

Summary of the Chapter

- The Sun gives us light and heat.
- Shadows are formed when something blocks the way of light.
- A shadow is formed on the opposite side of the source of light.
- Shadow keeps changing in length and direction.

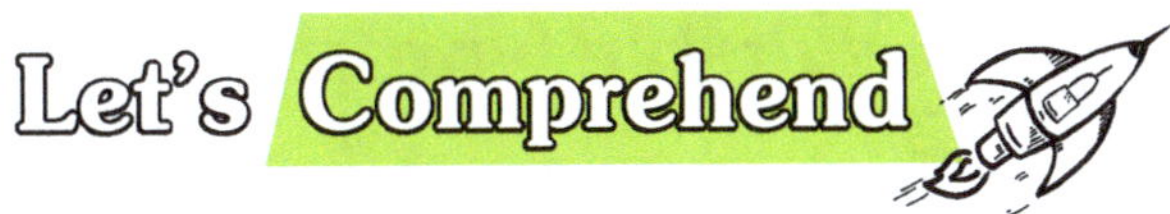

A. Answer the following questions :

1. What is the Sun?

2. What do we get from the Sun?

3. Why is Sunlight necessary for plants?

4. How is a shadow formed?

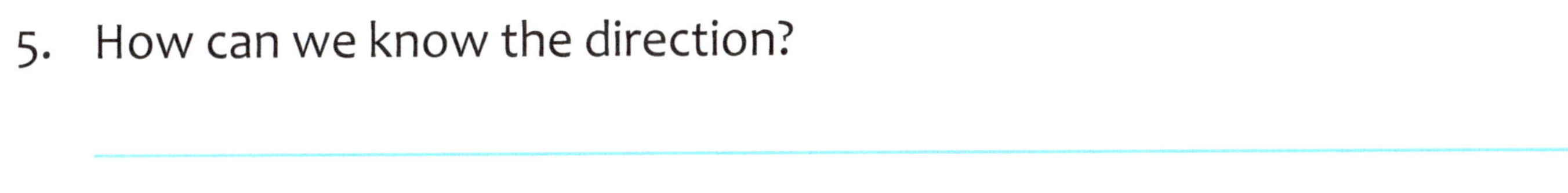

5. How can we know the direction?

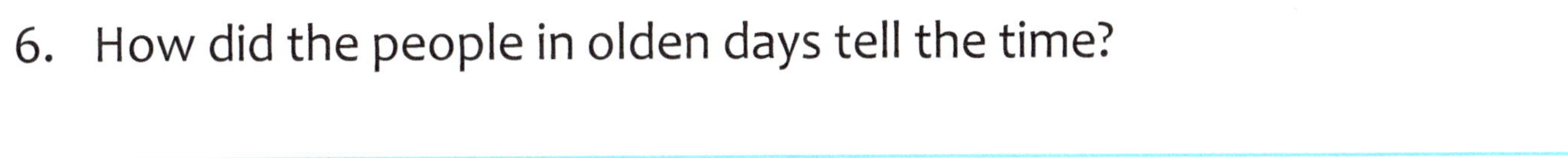

6. How did the people in olden days tell the time?

B. Fill in the blanks using the suitable words :

1. The Sun is a ____________ ball of ____________ .

2. Fruits ripen with the Sun's ____________ .

3. We work and play in ____________ .

4. Our left hand points towards the ____________ .

5. Shadows are very short at ____________ .

6. No shadow is formed in ____________ .

C. Tick (✓) the correct option:

1. The Sun is (far away from / near) the earth.

2. The Sun sets in the (east / west).

3. Days are (warm / cool).

4. Shadows always fall (on the opposite / the same) side of the light.

5. A shadow is formed when (nothing or something) comes in the way of light.

6. Light travels in a (straight / curved) line.

Get Hands-on Experience...

We must not look directly at the Sun. Our eyes can get damaged. Discuss it with your teacher.

Hands-on Learning...

Draw the outlines of the shapes of the Sun and its shadows seen by you on a sheet of white paper and cut them out with the help of your friends. Paste the cut-outs on a sheet of black paper. Show it to your teacher.

A. Answer the following questions :

1. Where do plants store food?

2. Why do climbers need support to stand?

3. What is protective food?

4. What should we do to make our muscles strong?

5. Write any three good food habits.

B. Fill in the blanks with the suitable words :

1. Wild animals live in a ___________ freely.

2. The Sun is a ___________ ball of ___________ .

3. ___________ have hard stems.

4. ___________ live in tree holes.

5. We should avoid ___________ food.

C. Match the following :

Column A	Column B
1. Lotus	a. framework of bones
2. Herb	b. water plant
3. Exercise	c. scavenger
4. Vulture	d. very small plant
5. Skeleton	e. strong bones and muscles

D. Write 'T' for a true statement and 'F' for a false one :

1. We should sit straight. ☐

2. Milk is not essential for good health. ☐

3. Plant-eating animals are called herbivorous animals. ☐

4. Muscles are not attached to bones.

5. Food is one of our basic needs.

E. Give two examples for each :

1. Protective food

2. Milk-giving animals

3. Omnivorous animals

4. Fruits from plants

5. Leaves that are eaten

F. Tick (✓) the correct answer :

1. They creep along the ground ____________ .

   a. Climbers ☐ b. Herbs ☐ c. Creepers ☐

2. These plants live only for one season ____________ .

   a. Climbers ☐ b. Herbs ☐ c. Creepers ☐

3. These plants can stand straight on the ground ____________ .

   a. Trees ☐ b. Creepers ☐ c. Shrubs ☐

4. These plants live for many years ____________ .

   a. Trees ☐ b. Shrubs ☐ c. Herbs ☐

5. These are used as hedges ____________ .

   a. Thorny plants ☐

   b. Creepers ☐

   c. Shrubs ☐

A.   Answer the following questions :

1.   Where can we find rocks on the earth?

2.   What are the three forms of water?

3.   Why does each of us need a house?

4.   What does the air contain?

5.   What are gemstones? Name any two gemstones.

B.   Fill in the blanks with the suitable words :

1.   ______________ is the main source of water.

2.   The ______________ is known as a pedestrian crossing.

3.   Our earth is made up of very big ______________ .

4.   The water itself is in ______________ form.

5.   Pucca houses are called ______________ houses.

C.   Match the following :

Column A	**Column B**
1. seeds	a. gentle and soft
2. wind	b. water vapour
3. water from clothes	c. carried to other places
4. breeze	d. fast and strong
5. storm	e. moving air

D.   Write 'T' for a true statement and 'F' for a false one :

1.   Drinking dirty water can make us feel sick.

2.   Steam is the gaseous form of water.

3. We should take a shower while bathing. ☐

4. Plants do not need water. ☐

5. The main sources of water are rivers and ponds. ☐

E. Give the names for the following :

1. Permanent House   ______________________

2. Temporary House   ______________________

3. House made of snow   ______________________

4. Moveable House   ______________________

F. Tick (✓) the correct answer :

1. Very strong moving air causes a ___________.

    a. wind ☐   b. breeze ☐   c. storm ☐

2. We should avoid playing with___________.

    a. badminton ☐

    b. dolls ☐

    c. sharp things ☐

3. Dust and smoke make the air___________.

    a. dirty ☐   b. clean ☐   c. fresh ☐

4. Dirty water makes us fall ___________.

    a. ill ☐   b. healthy ☐   c. weak ☐

5. The Sun rises in the___________.

    a. west ☐   b. east ☐   c. north ☐

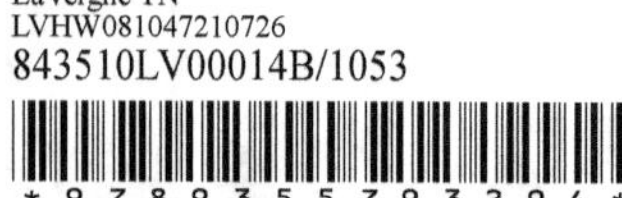
9 789355 793294